Cornhuskerology Trivia Challenge

Nebraska Cornhuskers Football

Cornhuskerology
Trivia
Challenge

Nebraska Cornhuskers Football

Researched by Billy G. Wilcox III

Paul F. Wilson & Tom P. Rippey III, Editors

Kick The Ball, Ltd
Lewis Center, Ohio

Trivia by Kick The Ball, Ltd

College Football Trivia

Alabama Crimson Tide	Auburn Tigers	Boston College Eagles	Florida Gators
Georgia Bulldogs	LSU Tigers	Miami Hurricanes	Michigan Wolverines
Nebraska Cornhuskers	Notre Dame Fighting Irish	Ohio State Buckeyes	Oklahoma Sooners
Oregon Ducks	Penn State Nittany Lions	Southern Cal Trojans	Texas Longhorns

Pro Football Trivia

Arizona Cardinals	Baltimore Ravens	Buffalo Bills	Chicago Bears
Cleveland Browns	Dallas Cowboys	Denver Broncos	Green Bay Packers
Indianapolis Colts	Kansas City Chiefs	Minnesota Vikings	New England Patriots
New Orleans Saints	New York Giants	New York Jets	Oakland Raiders
Philadelphia Eagles	Pittsburgh Steelers	San Francisco 49ers	Washington Redskins

Pro Baseball Trivia

Atlanta Braves	Baltimore Orioles	Boston Red Sox	Chicago Cubs
Chicago White Sox	Cincinnati Reds	Detroit Tigers	Houston Astros
Los Angeles Dodgers	Milwaukee Brewers	Minnesota Twins	New York Mets
New York Yankees	Philadelphia Phillies	Saint Louis Cardinals	San Francisco Giants

College Basketball Trivia

Duke Blue Devils	Georgetown Hoyas	Indiana Hoosiers	Kansas Jayhawks
Kentucky Wildcats	Maryland Terrapins	Michigan State Spartans	North Carolina Tar Heels
Syracuse Orange	UConn Huskies	UCLA Bruins	

Pro Basketball Trivia

Boston Celtics	Chicago Bulls	Detroit Pistons	Los Angeles Lakers
Utah Jazz			

Visit **www.TriviaGameBooks.com** for more details.

This book is dedicated to Brian Miller, Candace Books, Don and Sheri Miller, Ron and Lois Books, Tim and Jodi Holt, Jacob and Kaden Holt, Brad and Deanna Miller, Tyler, Traven and Tarynn Miller.

And to the world's friendliest fans at Memorial Stadium on game day, you made us feel like family when we visited your campus last season. Thank you for your unrivaled hospitality.

Cornhuskerology Trivia Challenge: Nebraska Cornhuskers Football; Third Edition 2012

Published by
Kick The Ball, Ltd
8595 Columbus Pike, Suite 197
Lewis Center, OH 43035
www.TriviaGameBooks.com

Edited by: Paul F. Wilson & Tom P. Rippey III
Designed and Formatted by: Paul F. Wilson
Researched by: Billy G. Wilcox III

Copyright © 2012 by Kick The Ball, Ltd, Lewis Center, Ohio

ALL RIGHTS RESERVED. No part of this book may be reproduced or transmitted in any form whatsoever, electronic, or mechanical, including photocopying, recording, or by any informational storage or retrieval system without the expressed written, dated and signed permission from the copyright holder.

Trademarks and Copyrights: Kick The Ball, Ltd is not associated with any event, team, conference, or league mentioned in this book. All trademarks are the property of their respective owners. Kick The Ball, Ltd respects and honors the copyrights and trademarks of others. We use event, team, conference, or league names only as points of reference in titles, questions, answers, and other sections of our trivia game books. Names, statistics, and others facts obtained through public domain resources.

LIMIT OF LIABILITY/DISCLAIMER OF WARRANTY: THE RESEARCHER AND PUBLISHER HAVE USED GREAT CARE IN RESEARCHING AND WRITING THIS BOOK. HOWEVER, WE MAKE NO REPRESENTATION OR WARRANTIES AS TO THE COMPLETENESS OF ITS CONTENTS OR THEIR ACCURACY AND WE SPECIFICALLY DISCLAIM ANY IMPLIED WARRANTIES OF MERCHANTABILITY OR FITNESS FOR A PARTICULAR PURPOSE. WARRANTIES MAY NOT BE CREATED OR EXTENDED BY ANY SALES MATERIALS OR SALESPERSON OF THIS BOOK. NEITHER THE RESEARCHER NOR THE PUBLISHER SHALL BE LIABLE FOR ANY LOSS OF PROFIT OR ANY OTHER COMMERCIAL DAMAGES, INCLUDING BUT NOT LIMITED TO SPECIAL, INCIDENTAL, CONSEQUENTIAL, OR OTHER DAMAGES.

For information on ordering this book in bulk at reduced prices, please email us at pfwilson@triviagamebooks.com.

International Standard Book Number: 978-1-613320-055-1
Printed and Bound in the United States of America
10 9 8 7 6 5 4 3 2 1

Table of Contents

Dear Friend,

Thank you for purchasing our *Cornhuskerology Trivia Challenge* game book!

We have made every attempt to verify the accuracy of the questions and answers contained in this book. However it is still possible that from time to time an error has been made by us or our researchers. In the event you find a question or answer that is questionable or inaccurate, we ask for your understanding and thank you for bringing it to our attention so we may improve future editions of this book. Please email us at tprippey@triviagamebooks.com with those observations and comments.

Have fun playing *Cornhuskerology Trivia Challenge*!

Paul & Tom

Paul Wilson and Tom Rippey
Co-Founders, Kick The Ball, Ltd

PS – You can discover more about all of our current trivia game books by visiting www.TriviaGameBooks.com.

Book Format:

There are four quarters, each made up of fifty questions. Each quarter's questions have assigned point values. Questions are designed to get progressively more difficult as you proceed through each quarter, as well as through the book itself. Most questions are in a four-option multiple-choice format so that you will at least have a 25 percent chance of getting a correct answer for some of the more challenging questions.

We have even added Overtime in the event of a tie, or just in case you want to keep playing a little longer.

Game Options:

One Player -
To play on your own, simply answer each of the questions in all the quarters, and in the overtime section, if you'd like. Use the Player / Team Score Sheet to record your answers and the quarter Answer Keys to check your answers. Calculate each quarter's points and the total for the game at the bottom of the Player / Team Score Sheet to determine your final score.

Two or More Players –
To play with multiple players decide if you will all be competing with each other individually, or if you will form and play as teams. Each player / team will then have its own Player / Team Score Sheet to record its answer. You can use the quarter Answer Keys to check your answers and to calculate your final scores.

The Player / Team Score Sheets have been designed so that each team can answer all questions or you can divide the questions up in any combination you would prefer. For example, you may want to alternate questions if two players are playing or answer every third question for three players, etc. In any case, simply record your response to your questions in the corresponding quarter and question number on the Player / Team Score Sheet.

A winner will be determined by multiplying the total number of correct answers for each quarter by the point value per quarter, then adding together the final total for all quarters combined. Play the game again and again by alternating the questions that your team is assigned so that you will answer a different set of questions each time you play.

You Create the Game -
There are countless other ways of using *Cornhuskerology Trivia Challenge* questions. It is limited only to your imagination. Examples might be using them at your tailgate or other college football related party. Players / Teams who answer questions incorrectly may have to perform a required action, or winners may receive special prizes. Let us know what other games you come up with!

Have fun!

1) What year did Nebraska adopt the Cornhusker nickname?

Answers begin on page 17

    A)   1894
    B)   1900
    C)   1918
    D)   1934

2) What are Nebraska's team colors?

    A)   Red and White
    B)   Crimson and White
    C)   Crimson and Cream
    D)   Scarlet and Cream

3) What is the name of the stadium where Nebraska plays?

    A)   Memorial Stadium
    B)   Husker Stadium
    C)   University Stadium
    D)   Lincoln Field

4) All time, how many Heisman Trophy winners played at Nebraska?

    A)   1
    B)   3
    C)   5
    D)   7

5) What is the nickname of Nebraska's marching band?

    A) Scarlet Symphony
    B) Husker Players
    C) Marching Red
    D) Red and White Express

6) What was awarded to the winner of the annual Nebraska-Missouri game?

    A) Bell
    B) Bucket
    C) Pitchfork
    D) Helmet

7) What is the name of the bronze statue that stands just east of Nebraska's stadium?

    A) Husker Nation Statue
    B) Statue of Champions
    C) Victory Statue
    D) Husker Legacy Statue

8) Who had the longest coaching tenure at Nebraska?

    A) Bob Devaney
    B) Dana X. Bible
    C) Tom Osborne
    D) Bill Glassford

9) Bernie Masterson had two stints as Nebraska's head coach.

    A) True
    B) False

10) Which Big Ten opponent has Nebraska played the most number of times?

    A) Penn State
    B) Minnesota
    C) Iowa
    D) Illinois

11) Who was the first-ever consensus All-American at Nebraska?

    A) Ed Weir
    B) Vic Halligan
    C) Guy Chamberlin
    D) George Sauer

12) Which Cornhusker was named 1988 Fiesta Bowl Defensive Player of the Game?

    A) Neil Smith
    B) Broderick Thomas
    C) Jim Skow
    D) Danny Noonan

13) What is the nickname of the Nebraska defense?

    A) Redshirts
    B) Blackshirts
    C) Red Swarm
    D) White Lightning

14) When was the last time the Nebraska defense led the nation in sacks?

    A) 1995
    B) 1997
    C) 2001
    D) 2005

15) The seating capacity for Memorial Stadium is greater than 85,000.

    A) True
    B) False

16) What year did Nebraska play its first-ever game?

    A) 1880
    B) 1890
    C) 1899
    D) 1903

17) Did Nebraska have over 2,500 yards passing in 2011?

    A) Yes
    B) No

18) Who was the first-ever Cornhusker to play in a Super Bowl?

    A) Kent McCloughan
    B) Monte Johnson
    C) Roger Craig
    D) Rik Bonness

19) Who holds the career rushing record at Nebraska?

    A) Ahman Green
    B) Lawrence Phillips
    C) Eric Crouch
    D) Mike Rozier

20) Who led Nebraska in tackles in 2011?

    A) Austin Cassidy
    B) Will Compton
    C) Lavonte David
    D) Cameron Meredith

21) Has any Cornhusker ever had 1,000 yards receiving in a single season?

    A) Yes
    B) No

22) Who did Nebraska defeat to earn their 500th all-time victory?

    A) Colorado Buffaloes
    B) Kansas Jayhawks
    C) Oklahoma Sooners
    D) Kansas State Wildcats

23) Who was Nebraska's first-ever Academic All-American?

    A) Jim Huge
    B) Rik Bonness
    C) Don Fricke
    D) Pat Clare

24) Who led Nebraska in rushing in Tom Osborne's first season as head coach?

    A) Jarvis Redwine
    B) I.M. Hipp
    C) Roger Craig
    D) Tony Davis

25) Who holds Nebraska's single-game record for the most passing yards?

- A) Turner Gill
- B) Joe Ganz
- C) Vince Ferragamo
- D) Zac Taylor

26) When was the last season Nebraska's leading passer had fewer than 1,000 yards?

- A) 1964
- B) 1975
- C) 1983
- D) 1998

27) How many former Nebraska head coaches are in the College Football Hall of Fame?

- A) 3
- B) 5
- C) 6
- D) 8

28) How many times has Nebraska started the season ranked No. 1 in the AP Poll?

- A) 6
- B) 8
- C) 11
- D) 14

29) When was the last season the Cornhuskers did not play in a bowl game?

  A) 1974
  B) 1980
  C) 2001
  D) 2007

30) What is the Huskers' record for the most yards rushing in a single game against Kansas?

  A) 385
  B) 476
  C) 567
  D) 753

31) How many Nebraska head coaches also played football for the Huskers?

  A) 2
  B) 4
  C) 5
  D) 6

32) Who is the only Nebraska QB to pass for more than 3,500 yards in a season?

  A) Tommie Frazier
  B) Zac Taylor
  C) Vince Ferragamo
  D) Joe Ganz

33) How many times has a No. 1-ranked Nebraska been beaten by an unranked opponent?

   A) 0
   B) 1
   C) 2
   D) 4

34) How many Nebraska players have had their jersey number retired?

   A) 3
   B) 5
   C) 7
   D) 9

35) Who is Nebraska's all-time leader in pass interceptions?

   A) Dana Stephenson
   B) Ralph Brown
   C) Josh Bullocks
   D) Bret Clark

36) Who has the longest TD run in Nebraska history?

   A) Ahman Green
   B) Calvin Jones
   C) Eric Crouch
   D) Tommie Frazier

37) Who is the only Husker to have over 400 career tackles?

    A) Trev Alberts
    B) Mike Brown
    C) Jerry Murtaugh
    D) Barrett Ruud

38) Which Nebraska I-Back had the most rushing attempts in a single game?

    A) Mike Rozier
    B) Cory Ross
    C) Tony Davis
    D) Lawrence Phillips

39) How many all-time bowl appearances has NU had?

    A) 40
    B) 44
    C) 48
    D) 52

40) In which year did Nebraska play its first-ever homecoming game?

    A) 1899
    B) 1902
    C) 1906
    D) 1911

41) How many AP National Championships has Nebraska been awarded?

    A) 2
    B) 4
    C) 5
    D) 7

42) What is the Huskers' all-time longest winning streak?

    A) 19 games
    B) 22 games
    C) 26 games
    D) 34 games

43) Who was the Huskers' first-ever opponent in Memorial Stadium?

    A) Oklahoma
    B) Iowa State
    C) Minnesota
    D) Missouri

44) How many outright conference titles has Nebraska won?

    A) 24
    B) 28
    C) 34
    D) 40

45) Who holds the Cornhuskers' single-game record for the most receiving yards?

    A) Irving Fryar
    B) Terrence Nunn
    C) Johnny Rodgers
    D) Matt Davison

46) What position did Barry Alvarez play at Nebraska?

    A) Center
    B) Linebacker
    C) Fullback
    D) Quarterback

47) How many Nebraska head coaches lasted only one season or less?

    A) 4
    B) 6
    C) 7
    D) 10

48) Who holds the Cornhuskers' record for the most points scored in a single game?

    A) Calvin Jones
    B) Eric Crouch
    C) Ahman Green
    D) Johnny Rodgers

49) Who holds Nebraska's career record for the most points scored?

    A)   Mike Rozier
    B)   Josh Brown
    C)   Kris Brown
    D)   Alex Henery

50) What year did Nebraska first celebrate a victory over Oklahoma?

    A)   1912
    B)   1929
    C)   1934
    D)   1941

Prior to 1900, Nebraska had several nicknames for their sports teams. They were known by such names as the Antelopes, Treeplanters and Bugeaters. Nebraska was also known as the Old Gold Knights for a while, but the nickname did not go with their school colors of scarlet and cream. In 1900, a Lincoln sportswriter came up with the nickname Cornhuskers. Although the term was once used to describe the University of Iowa, the name was quickly adopted and the rest is history.

1) B – 1900 (A Lincoln sportswriter first referred to the Nebraska football team as the Cornhuskers.)

2) D – Scarlet and Cream (These colors were adopted in 1892.)

3) A – Memorial Stadium (The Cornhuskers have played in Memorial Stadium since 1923. The Stadium's original seating capacity was 31,000.)

4) B – 3 (Johnny Rodgers won the Heisman in 1972, Mike Rozier in 1983 and Eric Crouch 2001.)

5) C – Marching Red

6) A – Bell (The tradition of using the Missouri-Nebraska Bell as a trophy began in 1927.)

7) D – Husker Legacy Statue (The statue was built in 1997 by Fred Hoppe.)

8) C – Tom Osborne (Osborne led the Cornhuskers for 25 seasons, 1973-97.)

9) B – False (George "Potsy" Clark is the only Nebraska coach to have had two coaching stints, in 1945 and again in 1948. Bernie Masterson coached the 1946-47 seasons in between Clark's two stints as head coach.)

10) B – Minnesota (Nebraska has played the Golden Gophers 52 times.)

11) B – Vic Halligan (1914)

12) A – Neil Smith (He was named Defensive Player of the Game as a defensive lineman, even though the Cornhuskers fell 28-31 to Florida State.)

13) B – Blackshirts (This nickname was first adopted in the 1960s because of the contrasting color of the practice jerseys.)

14) D – 2005 (The Cornhuskers finished with 50 team sacks for a 4.17 per game average.)

15) B – False (Official seating capacity is 81,067. However, plans are in place to expand to over 86,000 by 2013.)

16) B – 1890 (Nebraska defeated Omaha YMCA 10-0 in its first-ever official game.)

17) B – No (Nebraska completed 164 of 293 pass attempts for 2,115 yards in 2011.)

18) A – Kent McCloughan (He played for the Oakland Raiders in Super Bowl II vs. Green Bay.)

19) D – Mike Rozier (He gained 4,780 rushing yards from 1981-83.)

20) C – Lavonte David (David led the Nebraska defense with 133 tackles [65 solo] in 2011.)

21) B – No (The closest anyone has come to the 1,000-yard mark was Johnny Rodgers in 1972. He had 942 yards on 55 receptions.)

22) D – Kansas State Wildcats (51-0 in 1976)

23) C – Don Fricke (1960)

24) D – Tony Davis (He gained 1,008 yards on 254 carries in 1973.)

25) B – Joe Ganz (In 2007, he passed for 510 yards vs. Kansas State in a 73-31 win.)

26) D – 1998 (Bobby Newcombe led the Huskers with 712 yards passing.)

27) C – 6 (Fielding Yost, E.N. Robinson, Dana X. Bible, Bob Devaney, Lawrence McCeney "Biff" Jones and Tom Osborne)

28) A – 6 (1965, 1972, 1976, 1983, 1996 and 2000)

29) D – 2007 (Nebraska finished with a 5-7 record.)

30) C – 567 (The Cornhuskers ran over the Jayhawks in 1983 [Nebraska 67, Kansas 13].)

31) B – 4 (Glenn Presnell, Adolph J. Lewandowski, Bernie Masterson and Frank Solich)

32) D – Joe Ganz (Ganz passed for 3,568 yards in 2008.)

33) C – 2 (Top-ranked Nebraska fell 17-20 at UCLA in 1972 and 9-17 at Syracuse in 1984.)

34) A – 3 (Johnny Rodgers [#20], Tom Novak [#60] and Bob Brown [#64] are the only Huskers to have their number retired. Nebraska usually retires a player's jersey itself rather than his number.)

35) A – Dana Stephenson (He recorded 14 career interceptions from1967-69.)

36) C – Eric Crouch (Crouch had a 95-yard TD run vs. Missouri in 2001 [Nebraska 36, Missouri 3].)

37) D – Barrett Ruud (He recorded 432 career tackles from 2001-04.)

38) B – Cory Ross (He carried the ball 37 times for 138 yards in a 17-3 victory vs. Michigan State in the 2003 Alamo Bowl.)

39) C – 48 (Nebraska has appeared in 48 bowl games and has an all-time record of 24-24.)

40) D – 1911 (Nebraska battled Michigan to a 6-6 tie on Nov. 23.)

41) B – 4 (1970, 1971, 1994 and 1995; Nebraska was No. 1 in the 1997 Coaches Poll, however, Michigan was No. 1 in the AP Poll.)

42) C – 26 games (Nebraska won every game from Aug. 28, 1994, a 31-0 victory over West Virginia until losing on Sept. 21, 1996, a 0-19 loss to Arizona State.)

43) A – Oklahoma (Nebraska beat the Sooners 24-0 on Oct. 13, 1923.)

44) C – 34 (Nebraska has won 34 outright titles and shared nine more.)

45) D – Matt Davison (He gained 167 yards on 10 catches at Texas A&M in 1998 [Nebraska 21, Texas A&M 28].)

46) B – Linebacker (Alvarez was a three-year starter at Nebraska from 1965-67.)

47) C – 7 (Charles Thomas 1895, Fielding Yost 1898, A. Edwin Branch 1899, Amos Foster 1906, William G. Kline 1918, Glenn Presnell 1942 and Pete Elliott 1956)

48) A – Calvin Jones (He scored 36 points on six TDS at Kansas in 1991 [Nebraska 59, Kansas 23].)

49) D – Alex Henery (Henery scored 397 points during his Nebraska career [2007-10].)

50) A – 1912 (Nebraska 13, Oklahoma 9)

Note: All answers are valid as of the end of the 2011 season, unless otherwise indicated in the question itself.

1) Who holds Nebraska's record for the most rushing yards in a bowl game?

Answers begin on page 37

    A) Keith Jones
    B) Ken Clark
    C) Mike Rozier
    D) Dan Alexander

2) Who holds NU's record for the most pass receptions in a game?

    A) Matt Davison
    B) Dennis Richnafsky
    C) Johnny Rodgers
    D) Freeman White

3) How many Nebraska defensive players are in the College Football Hall of Fame?

    A) 3
    B) 5
    C) 7
    D) 9

4) How many decades have the Huskers won at least 85 games?

    A) 1
    B) 3
    C) 4
    D) 6

5) What year was the first-ever undefeated and untied season for Nebraska (minimum 8 games)?

- A) 1902
- B) 1916
- C) 1928
- D) 1932

6) How many undefeated and untied seasons has Nebraska had (minimum 8 games)?

- A) 3
- B) 5
- C) 8
- D) 10

7) How many undefeated seasons with one tie has Nebraska had (minimum 8 games)?

- A) 0
- B) 2
- C) 4
- D) 7

8) Who led Nebraska in pass receptions in 2011?

- A) Rex Burkhead
- B) Kenny Bell
- C) Brandon Kinnie
- D) Quincy Enunwa

9) Which U.S. Service Academy has Nebraska never played?

    A) Navy
    B) Army
    C) Air Force
    D) Has Played All Three

10) Who led the Cornhuskers in quarterback sacks in 2011?

    A) Cameron Meredith
    B) Eric Martin
    C) Will Compton
    D) Lavonte David

11) Ndamukong Suh was named the AP College Football Player of the Year in 2009.

    A) True
    B) False

12) What is Nebraska's record for the most passes attempted in a single game?

    A) 42
    B) 49
    C) 58
    D) 67

13) What is Nebraska's record for the most passes completed in a single game?

   A) 32
   B) 37
   C) 41
   D) 47

14) What year was the first-ever Nebraska-Kansas game?

   A) 1892
   B) 1906
   C) 1917
   D) 1926

15) Who holds the record for the longest kickoff return in Nebraska history?

   A) Johnny Rodgers
   B) Frank Solich
   C) Cory Ross
   D) Owen Frank

16) Since 1965, who is the only Cornhusker to lead the team in rushing for three straight seasons?

   A) Jarvis Redwine
   B) Mike Rozier
   C) Ahman Green
   D) Doug DuBose

17) Which Husker holds the NCAA record for the most field goals made in a game?

A) Gregg Barrios
B) Dale Klein
C) Josh Brown
D) Kris Brown

18) Which lineman scored the touchdown on the famous Fumblerooski play in the 1984 Orange Bowl?

A) Dean Steinkuhler
B) Harry Grimminger
C) Dave Rimington
D) John McCormick

19) Which QB holds Nebraska's record for the most consecutive pass attempts without an interception?

A) Dave Humm
B) Turner Gill
C) Jerry Tagge
D) Scott Frost

20) All time, the Huskers have won more bowl games than any other school.

A) True
B) False

21) Who was Nebraska's first-ever bowl opponent?

    A) Alabama
    B) Penn State
    C) Stanford
    D) Miami

22) Tom Osborne lost his first bowl game as head coach at Nebraska.

    A) True
    B) False

23) Which QB holds the Nebraska record for the most passing yards in a bowl game?

    A) Joe Ganz
    B) Turner Gill
    C) Tommie Frazier
    D) Dave Humm

24) What are the most home games Nebraska has lost in one season?

    A) 3
    B) 4
    C) 5
    D) 6

25) Which school was the first to beat Nebraska in the Tom Osborne era?

   A) Wisconsin
   B) Missouri
   C) Kansas State
   D) Oklahoma

26) Who defeated NU in Tom Osborne's first home loss?

   A) Kansas
   B) Oklahoma
   C) Colorado
   D) Minnesota

27) How many straight years did Tom Osborne lead Nebraska to a bowl game?

   A) 14
   B) 18
   C) 21
   D) 25

28) How many Orange Bowls did Tom Osborne lead Nebraska to?

   A) 5
   B) 8
   C) 10
   D) 13

29) Who holds NU's record for the most career blocked punts?

    A)   Ralph Brown
    B)   Grant Wistrom
    C)   Barron Miles
    D)   Daniel Bullocks

30) What was the highest AP ranking the Cornhuskers achieved in 2011?

    A)   No. 5
    B)   No. 8
    C)   No. 11
    D)   No. 14

31) Which Cornhusker holds the school record for the most career touchdown receptions?

    A)   Johnny Rodgers
    B)   Irving Fryar
    C)   Matt Davison
    D)   Nate Swift

32) Which Husker held the NCAA record for rushing yards by a QB in a bowl game?

    A)   Eric Crouch
    B)   Turner Gill
    C)   Scott Frost
    D)   Tommie Frazier

33) What are the most consecutive weeks Nebraska has held the AP's No. 1 ranking during the regular season?

    A) 10
    B) 12
    C) 15
    D) 17

34) What team was the last to defeat the Huskers in a bowl game?

    A) Washington
    B) Miami
    C) Auburn
    D) South Carolina

35) Bob Devaney led Nebraska to its first-ever bowl game victory.

    A) True
    B) False

36) What is the longest pass play in Nebraska history?

    A) 87 yards
    B) 91 yards
    C) 95 yards
    D) 99 yards

37) Tommie Frazier passed for more career yards at Nebraska than Turner Gill.

    A) True
    B) False

38) How many three-time consensus All-Americans does Nebraska have?

    A) 0
    B) 2
    C) 4
    D) 5

39) Has a Nebraska I-Back ever rushed for more than 2,000 yards in a single season?

    A) Yes
    B) No

40) How many Nebraska I-Backs have over 3,000 career rushing yards?

    A) 2
    B) 3
    C) 4
    D) 5

41) Who holds Nebraska's record for the most consecutive passes completed?

    A) Zac Taylor
    B) Vince Ferragamo
    C) Dave Humm
    D) Jerry Tagge

42) Who holds the NU record for the most receptions in a season?

    A) Matt Davison
    B) Johnny Rodgers
    C) Nate Swift
    D) Marlon Lucky

43) Which NU tight end has the most career TD catches?

    A) Johnny Mitchell
    B) Junior Miller
    C) Tracey Wistrom
    D) Todd Millikan

44) How many outright Big 8 Championships did Nebraska win?

    A) 12
    B) 15
    C) 18
    D) 21

45) How many times did Nebraska share the Big 8 Title with Oklahoma?

    A) 2
    B) 3
    C) 5
    D) 7

46) Against which conference opponent does Nebraska have the most wins?

    A) Iowa
    B) Minnesota
    C) Northwestern
    D) Michigan State

47) What conference opponent has the most wins against Nebraska?

    A) Penn State
    B) Iowa
    C) Minnesota
    D) Indiana

48) Nebraska has a .750 all-time winning percentage in Memorial Stadium.

    A) True
    B) False

49) When was the last time Nebraska played a non-sellout game at Memorial Stadium?

    A)   1956
    B)   1962
    C)   1971
    D)   1979

50) What year did Nebraska win its first-ever outright conference title?

    A)   1902
    B)   1908
    C)   1910
    D)   1917

On Jan. 1, 1973, over 80,000 fans piled into the Orange Bowl to watch the Cornhuskers defeat Notre Dame 40-6 in Bob Devaney's final game as Nebraska's head coach. In that game, Heisman Trophy winner Johnny Rodgers proved why he was chosen as the best player in the nation with a performance that will go down in Nebraska and Orange Bowl history as one of the greatest ever. Rodgers had touchdown runs of eight, four and five yards; caught a 50-yard touchdown pass from quarterback Dave Humm; and threw a 52-yard touchdown pass to Frosty Anderson. In doing so, Rodgers became the first-ever player in Nebraska history to run, pass and throw for a touchdown in the same game. Believe it or not, Rodgers was able to accomplish this historic feat despite being pulled from the game with six minutes left in the third quarter.

1) D – Dan Alexander (Alexander rushed for 240 yards in a 66-17 win over Northwestern in the 2000 Alamo Bowl.)

2) B – Dennis Richnafsky (Richnafsky had 14 catches for 145 yards in a 16-14 win at Kansas State in 1967.)

3) A – 3 (Wayne Meylan [LB], Rich Glover [MG] and Grant Wistrom [DE])

4) B – 3 (1970s, 1980s and 1990s)

5) A – 1902 (Nebraska went 9-0-0 in 1902 and did not give up a single point.)

6) C – 8 (1902, 1903, 1913, 1915, 1971, 1994, 1995 and 1997)

7) B – 2 (1914 and 1970)

8) B – Kenny Bell (Bell caught 32 passes for 461 yards and three TDs in 2011.)

9) A – Navy

10) D – Lavonte David (David led the Cornhuskers with 5.5 sacks in 2011.)

11) A – True (Suh is the first Nebraska player to win the prestigious award.)

12) C – 58 (Joe Ganz was 31-58 for 484 yards in a 65-51 loss to Colorado in 2007.)

13) B – 37 (Nebraska completed 37 of 45 attempts for 357 yards at Texas Tech in 2008.)

14) A – 1892 (Kansas beat Nebraska 12-0 in Lincoln in 1892.)

15) D – Owen Frank (Owen had a 105-yard TD return vs. Kansas State in 1911 [NU 59, Kansas State 0].)

16) C – Ahman Green (1995-97)

17) B – Dale Klein (Klein was seven for seven in a 28-20 win at Missouri in 1985.)

18) A – Dean Steinkuhler (The All-American rumbled 19 yards for a TD vs. Miami. Miami still won the game 31-30.)

19) D – Scott Frost (Frost did not throw an interception in 155 attempts over a 9-game period between November 1996 and October 1997.)

20) B – False (Nebraska has 24 bowl wins which ranks them eighth all time.)

21) C – Stanford (1941 Rose Bowl [Nebraska 13, Stanford 21])

22) B – False (Nebraska beat Texas 19-3 in the 1974 Cotton Bowl.)

23) A – Joe Ganz (Ganz threw for 236 yards versus Clemson in the 2009 Gator Bowl.)

24) C – 5 (It has happened on three occasions: 1947, 1951 and 1957.)

25) B – Missouri (Nebraska lost 12-13 at Missouri on Oct. 13, 1973.)

26) B – Oklahoma (The Sooners shut out Nebraska, 0-27, on Nov. 23, 1973.)

27) D – 25 (Osborne led Nebraska to a bowl game every year from 1973-97.)

28) C – 10 (Osborne led Nebraska to 10 Orange Bowls, with an overall 3-7 record.)

29) C – Barron Miles (He blocked seven punts during his career at Nebraska, from 1992-94.)

30) B – No. 8 (Nebraska was ranked No. 8 in the country before losing to Wisconsin on Oct. 1.)

31) A – Johnny Rodgers (Rodgers had 25 touchdown receptions in his Nebraska career, from 1970-72.)

32) D – Tommie Frazier (Frazier rushed for 199 yards vs. Florida in the 1996 Fiesta Bowl. Nebraska won the game 62-28, its second straight National Championship. Vince Young broke the record by rushing for 200 yards in the 2006 Rose Bowl.)

33) B – 12 (This happened on two occasions: from Sept. 18, 1971, to Sept. 9, 1972, and again from Aug. 29, 1983, to Nov. 26, 1983.)

34) D – South Carolina (Nebraska lost 13-30 to South Carolina in the 2012 Capital One Bowl.)

35) A – True (Devaney led NU to a 36-34 win over Miami in the 1962 Gotham Bowl in New York.)

36) C – 95 yards (Fred Duda threw a 95-yard TD pass to Freeman White in a 38-13 win vs. Colorado in 1965.)

37) A – True (Frazier threw for 3,521 yards while Gill finished with 3,317 yards.)

38) A – 0 (The Huskers have never had a three-time consensus First Team All-American.)

39) A – Yes (Mike Rozier rushed for 2,148 yards on 275 attempts in 1983.)

40) D – 5 (Mike Rozier [4,780], Ahman Green [3,880], Roy Helu Jr. [3,404], Calvin Jones [3,153] and Ken Clark [3,112])

41) C – Dave Humm (Humm completed 15 straight passes at Kansas in 1974, a 56-0 Nebraska win.)

42) D – Marlon Lucky (Lucky had 75 receptions for the Huskers in 2007.)

43) D – Todd Millikan (Millikan had 14 TD catches for Nebraska from 1985-88.)

44) B – 15 (Nebraska won 15 Big 8 Titles outright and shared five more.)

45) B – 3 (Nebraska and Oklahoma shared the title three times [1975, 1978 and 1984].)

46) A – Iowa (Nebraska has 27 all-time wins vs. the Hawkeyes.)

47) C – Minnesota (The Huskers have lost 29 games to the Golden Gophers.)

48) A – True (The Huskers have a 384-117-13 record [.760] at Memorial Stadium since 1923.)

49) B – 1962 (The last non-sellout game at Memorial Stadium was on Oct. 20, 1962.)

50) C – 1910 (W.C. Cole led Nebraska to a 7-1-0 record and the Missouri Valley Conference Title.)

Note: All answers are valid as of the end of the 2011 season, unless otherwise indicated in the question itself.

1) What song plays as the Huskers make their way to the field at Memorial Stadium?

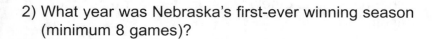

Answers begin on page 56

    A)   "Welcome to the Jungle"
    B)   "Seek and Destroy"
    C)   "Sirius"
    D)   "We Will Rock You"

2) What year was Nebraska's first-ever winning season (minimum 8 games)?

    A)   1894
    B)   1897
    C)   1906
    D)   1912

3) What year was Nebraska's first-ever 10-win season?

    A)   1899
    B)   1903
    C)   1914
    D)   1921

4) What year was the first-ever conference game between Nebraska and Kansas State?

    A)   1901
    B)   1910
    C)   1913
    D)   1919

5) What are the most points scored in a single game by the Huskers?

    A) 76
    B) 80
    C) 97
    D) 119

6) Nebraska has had a player gain over 500 yards rushing every year since 1963.

    A) True
    B) False

7) Which quarterback led the Huskers in rushing for two straight seasons?

    A) Eric Crouch
    B) Tommie Frazier
    C) Jammal Lord
    D) Scott Frost

8) What year did the 'N' first appear on the sides of Nebraska's helmet?

    A) 1955
    B) 1961
    C) 1970
    D) 1973

9) Who was the first black player to play for Nebraska?

- A) George Flippin
- B) Freeman White
- C) William Johnson
- D) Robert Taylor

10) What is the largest crowd to ever see a Nebraska football game?

- A) 108,106
- B) 110,962
- C) 113,718
- D) 115,039

11) The attendance record for a football game at Memorial Stadium is over 86,000.

- A) True
- B) False

12) How many points did Nebraska score in the 1983 season?

- A) 562
- B) 580
- C) 599
- D) 624

13) What is Nebraska's record for the most tackles for loss in one season?

A) 19
B) 25
C) 28
D) 33

14) Who has the most career fumble recoveries at Nebraska?

A) Ron Pruitt
B) Mike Brown
C) Broderick Thomas
D) Trev Alberts

15) Nebraska led the Big Ten in rushing yards in 2011.

A) True
B) False

16) Which team handed Nebraska its largest margin of defeat of all time?

A) Notre Dame
B) Oklahoma
C) Kansas State
D) Texas Tech

17) Who was the most recent Cornhusker to lead the team in rushing yards and pass receptions in the same season?

    A) Calvin Jones
    B) Mike Rozier
    C) Marlon Lucky
    D) Ahman Green

18) What is the song the Nebraska band plays after a TD?

    A) "Hail Varsity"
    B) "Victory March"
    C) "Fight On"
    D) "Husker Battle Song"

19) What is Nebraska's team record for the most defensive pass interceptions in a game?

    A) 5
    B) 7
    C) 9
    D) 11

20) What is the longest field goal ever kicked against Nebraska?

    A) 49 yards
    B) 55 yards
    C) 61 yards
    D) 65 yards

21) How many Huskers were drafted in the first round of the NFL Draft in the entire decade of the 1990s?

   A) 5
   B) 8
   C) 11
   D) 14

22) Who was Nebraska's opponent, to decide the National Champion, in the 1995 Orange Bowl?

   A) Virginia Tech
   B) Florida
   C) Florida State
   D) Miami

23) How many times has NU met Florida State in a bowl game?

   A) 2
   B) 4
   C) 6
   D) 8

24) Who was the first-ever black player named consensus All-American at Nebraska?

   A) Johnny Rodgers
   B) Freeman White
   C) Bob Brown
   D) Willie Harper

25) Nebraska has more offensive linemen than running backs in the College Football Hall of Fame.

   A) True
   B) False

26) Who was the first consensus All-American defensive player for the Huskers?

   A) Jerry Murtaugh
   B) Rich Glover
   C) Larry Wachholtz
   D) Wayne Meylan

27) How many times were Husker players named consensus All-Americans under Coach Bill Callahan?

   A) 0
   B) 2
   C) 3
   D) 5

28) In which decade were the most Nebraska players named consensus All-American?

   A) 1950s
   B) 1970s
   C) 1980s
   D) 1990s

29) How many Nebraska players have been named consensus All-Americans more than once?

    A) 5
    B) 7
    C) 9
    D) 12

30) Has any Nebraska player been named consensus All-American at two different positions?

    A) Yes
    B) No

31) What school did Nebraska play three times in the 1891 regular season?

    A) Iowa
    B) Illinois
    C) Doane College
    D) Nebraska Wesleyan

32) How many Nebraska players have finished second in Heisman voting?

    A) 2
    B) 4
    C) 6
    D) 7

33) Who is the only Nebraska player to be named Big 8 Defensive Player of the Year twice?

    A) Trev Alberts
    B) Rich Glover
    C) Broderick Thomas
    D) Jimmy Williams

34) What is the record for the most points ever allowed by the Cornhuskers?

    A) 58
    B) 63
    C) 70
    D) 76

35) What are the most consecutive conference titles won by the Cornhuskers?

    A) 1
    B) 3
    C) 5
    D) 7

36) What are NU's most consecutive bowl losses?

    A) 3
    B) 5
    C) 7
    D) 9

37) Has Nebraska ever played overtime in a bowl game?

    A) Yes
    B) No

38) Where did Nebraska play before moving to Memorial Stadium?

    A) Nebraska Field
    B) Cornhusker Stadium
    C) Lincoln Park
    D) Huskers' Field

39) All time, how many times has Nebraska shut out an opponent?

    A) 178
    B) 243
    C) 286
    D) 314

40) What are the most points Nebraska scored in a game in 2011?

    A) 43
    B) 47
    C) 51
    D) 55

41) What is Nebraska's record for the most consecutive bowl game victories?

    A) 3
    B) 5
    C) 6
    D) 8

42) How many total points per game did the 1971 Nebraska National Championship team allow?

    A) 4.1
    B) 5.4
    C) 6.9
    D) 8.0

43) Who led NU in their first-ever game at Memorial Stadium?

    A) Fred Dawson
    B) Dana X. Bible
    C) E.J. 'Doc' Stewart
    D) Glenn Presnell

44) Who did Nebraska defeat for their last Big 12 Conference win?

    A) Oklahoma
    B) Colorado
    C) Iowa State
    D) Kansas

45) How many yards per carry did Mike Rozier average in his career at Nebraska?

   A) 4.92
   B) 5.57
   C) 6.00
   D) 7.16

46) Has Nebraska ever lost nine games in a season?

   A) Yes
   B) No

47) Who was the first Husker football player to appear on the cover of *Sports Illustrated*?

   A) Johnny Rodgers
   B) Bob Terrio
   C) Jerry Hagge
   D) Frank Solich

48) Who was the first-ever Cornhusker to be chosen No. 1 overall in the NFL Draft?

   A) Bob Brown
   B) Junior Miller
   C) Sam Francis
   D) Johnny Rodgers

49) Who holds the all-time record for the most rushing touchdowns in a career at Nebraska?

A) Mike Rozier
B) Ahman Green
C) Tommie Frazier
D) Eric Crouch

50) Who did Nebraska beat for their 700th win?

A) Kansas
B) Kansas State
C) Oklahoma
D) Missouri

With Nebraska trailing Miami 17-0 in the 1984 Orange Bowl, Tom Osborne called one of the most well known plays in the history of college football. QB Turner Gill took the snap from center and set the ball on the ground in front of him, creating a "fumble." As Gill and the rest of the backfield ran right, right guard Dean Steinkuhler scooped up the ball and ran 19 yards to the left corner of the end zone for a touchdown. The play was called the Fumblerooski and was considered so deceitful that the NCAA banned intentional fumbles from college football after the 1992 season.

1) C – "Sirius" (Alan Parsons Project)
2) A – 1894 (Nebraska posted a 6-2 record in 1894 under Coach Frank Crawford.)
3) B – 1903 (Nebraska was 10-0 in 1903 under Coach W.C. "Bummy" Booth.)
4) C – 1913 (24-6 win in the Missouri Valley Conference)
5) D – 119 (Nebraska beat Haskell 119-0 in 1910.)
6) B – False (Frank Solich led the Huskers in rushing with 444 yards in 1964.)
7) C – Jammal Lord (1,412 yards in 2002 and 948 yards in 2003)
8) D – 1970 (Nebraska previously wore their jersey numbers on their helmets. They then used "NU" before using the single "N.")
9) A – George Flippin (1891-94)
10) C – 113,718 (Nebraska played in front of 113,718 fans at Michigan in 2011.)
11) A – True (86,304 fans piled into Memorial Stadium to watch the Cornhuskers beat Louisiana Lafayette 55-0 in 2009.)
12) D – 624 (Nebraska scored an NCAA record 624 points in 1983.)
13) B – 25 (Jim Skow, 1985)
14) A – Ron Pruitt (Pruitt had nine fumble recoveries for Nebraska from 1973-76.)
15) B – False (Nebraska rushed for 2,824 yards in 2011, finishing third in the Big Ten Conference.)

16) D – Texas Tech (Tech rolled to a 70-10 home victory against NU in 2004.)

17) C – Marlon Lucky (Lucky rushed for 1,019 yards and caught 75 passes in 2007.)

18) A – "Hail Varsity"

19) B – 7 (Nebraska intercepted seven passes versus Kansas State in 1970 [Nebraska 51, Kansas State 13].)

20) C – 61 yards (Mark Potter's 61-yard boot accounted for Kansas State's only points in a 48-3 loss to Nebraska in 1988.)

21) B – 8 (DB Bruce Pickens 1991, LB Mike Croel 1991, TE Johnny Mitchell 1992, LB Trev Alberts 1994, RB Lawrence Phillips 1996, CB Michael Booker 1997, DE Grant Wistrom 1991 and DT Jason Peter 1998)

22) D – Miami (Nebraska defeated Miami 24-17 to win their third National Championship.)

23) B – 4 (Nebraska faced Florida State in the 1988 and 1990 Fiesta Bowls and 1993 and 1994 Orange Bowls. Florida State won all four.)

24) C – Bob Brown (Brown became Nebraska's first black All-American following the 1963 season.)

25) A – True (With the addition of Will Shields in 2011, Nebraska now has five offensive linemen and four running backs in the College Football Hall of Fame.)

26) D – Wayne Meylan (Middle guard, 1966 and 1967)

27) A – 0

28) C – 1980s (Nebraska had 13 players named consensus All-American during the 1980s.)

29) C – 9 (Ed Weir 1924-25, Wayne Meylan 1966-67, Willie Harper 1971-72, Johnny Rodgers 1971-72, Dave Rimington 1981-82, Mike Rozier 1982-83, Jake Young 1988-89, Aaron Taylor 1996-97 and Grant Wistrom 1996-97)

30) A – Yes (Aaron Taylor was an All-American at center in 1996 and guard in 1997.)

31) C – Doane College (Nebraska only played four games that year, three of them were against Doane, going 2-1 in those matchups. The other game was a 22-0 loss to Iowa.)

32) A – 2 (FB Sam Francis in 1936 and QB Tommie Frazier in 1995)

33) B – Rich Glover (Glover was named Big 8 Defensive Player of the Year in 1971 and 1972.)

34) D – 76 (Nebraska gave up 76 points to Kansas in 2007 [Nebraska 38, Kansas 76].)

35) C – 5 (Nebraska won five straight Big 8 Titles from 1991-95.)

36) C – 7 (Nebraska lost in the 1988 Fiesta Bowl, 1989 Orange Bowl, 1990 Fiesta Bowl, 1991 Citrus Bowl, and 1992,1993 and 1994 Orange Bowls.)

37) B – No (Nebraska has never played in an overtime bowl game.)

38) A – Nebraska Field (Nebraska played at Nebraska Field [capacity 10,000] from 1909-22.)

39) C – 286 (Nebraska has shut out their opponent 286 times; most recently a 33-0 victory over Arizona in the 2009 Holiday Bowl.)

40) C – 51 (Nebraska beat Washington 51-38.)

41) C – 6 (Nebraska won the 1969 Sun Bowl, 1971, 1972 and 1973 Orange Bowls, 1974 Cotton Bowl and 1974 Sugar Bowl.)

42) D – 8.0 (Nebraska allowed only 104 points in 13 games, including three shutouts.)

43) A – Fred Dawson (Dawson coached Nebraska in their first game at Memorial Stadium.)

44) B – Colorado (Nebraska beat Colorado 45-17 in 2010 for their last Big 12 Conference win.)

45) D – 7.16 (Rozier averaged 7.16 yards per carry as a Cornhusker.)

46) A – Yes (Nebraska went 1-9-0 in 1957 under first year coach Bill Jennings.)

47) D – Frank Solich (Solich appeared on the cover of *Sports Illustrated* on Sept. 20, 1965.)

48) C – Sam Francis (The FB was drafted No. 1 overall by Philadelphia in 1937.)

49) D – Eric Crouch (Crouch rushed for 59 touchdowns from 1998-2001, setting an NCAA record for quarterbacks.)

50) B – Kansas State (Nebraska beat KSU 39-3 at Kansas State Oct. 5, 1996)

Note: All answers are valid as of the end of the 2011 season, unless otherwise indicated in the question itself.

1) Which school has Nebraska never beaten?

Answers begin on page 75

    A)   Michigan
    B)   USC
    C)   Washington
    D)   West Virginia

2) How many interceptions did the Nebraska defense record in 2011?

    A)   10
    B)   11
    C)   12
    D)   13

3) How many Big 8 Titles did Nebraska win under Coach Bob Devaney?

    A)   6
    B)   7
    C)   8
    D)   9

4) How many bowl games did Nebraska win under Coach Bob Devaney?

    A)   2
    B)   4
    C)   6
    D)   8

5) What number did Irving Fryar wear at Nebraska?

A) 22
B) 27
C) 33
D) 45

6) How many total points did Nebraska score in 2011?

A) 379
B) 392
C) 413
D) 428

7) Which Husker quarterback rushed for the most yards in a single game?

A) Eric Crouch
B) Tommie Frazier
C) Jammal Lord
D) Taylor Martinez

8) What year did Nebraska play their first-ever indoor game?

A) 1971
B) 1976
C) 1983
D) 1990

9) Which Husker recorded the most total tackles in a single game?

    A) Barrett Ruud
    B) Demorrio Williams
    C) Lee Kunz
    D) Clete Pillen

10) When was the last time the Huskers were shut out?

    A) 1989
    B) 1992
    C) 1996
    D) 2000

11) Which team passed for the most yards in a game against the Nebraska defense?

    A) Louisiana Tech
    B) Miami
    C) Colorado
    D) Texas Tech

12) How many times did Nebraska shut out their opponents under Coach Tom Osborne?

    A) 27
    B) 35
    C) 41
    D) 46

13) How many times was Tom Osborne named AP Big 8 Coach of the Year?

A) 2
B) 4
C) 5
D) 7

14) Who holds Nebraska's single-season rushing record?

A) Mike Rozier
B) Eric Crouch
C) Ahman Green
D) Cory Ross

15) Has Nebraska ever had four players rush for over 100 yards in the same game?

A) Yes
B) No

16) Who was Mike Rozier's fullback during his Heisman Trophy-winning season at Nebraska?

A) Tom Rathman
B) Andra Franklin
C) Ken Kaelin
D) Mark Schellen

17) Who holds the NU freshman single-season rushing record?

    A)   Lawrence Phillips
    B)   Ahman Green
    C)   Calvin Jones
    D)   Mike Rozier

18) In what year did Nebraska make its first-ever Orange Bowl appearance?

    A)   1947
    B)   1955
    C)   1962
    D)   1971

19) How many times in his Nebraska career did Mike Rozier rush for 100 yards in a game?

    A)   21
    B)   26
    C)   30
    D)   33

20) Who is the only Cornhusker linebacker to win the Butkus Award?

    A)   Trev Alberts
    B)   Barrett Ruud
    C)   Broderick Thomas
    D)   Ed Stewart

21) All time, how many head coaches has Nebraska had?

    A) 20
    B) 24
    C) 28
    D) 30

22) Which coach has the highest overall winning percentage at Nebraska (minimum 3 seasons)?

    A) Bob Devaney
    B) Dana X. Bible
    C) Tom Osborne
    D) E.O. Stiehm

23) Which coaches are second and third for the highest winning percentage at Nebraska?

    A) Bob Devaney and Tom Osborne
    B) Bob Devaney and Frank Solich
    C) W.C. Booth and Tom Osborne
    D) Frank Solich and Dana X. Bible

24) How many overtime games did the Huskers play in 2011?

    A) 0
    B) 1
    C) 2
    D) 3

25) How many career receptions did Eric Crouch have at Nebraska?

    A) 0
    B) 2
    C) 3
    D) 5

26) Does Nebraska have more than 800 all-time wins?

    A) Yes
    B) No

27) Who is the only Nebraska quarterback to be drafted in the first round of the NFL Draft?

    A) Dave Humm
    B) Vince Ferragamo
    C) Tommie Frazier
    D) Jerry Tagge

28) What decade did Nebraska have the highest winning percentage (minimum 50 games)?

    A) 1920s
    B) 1960s
    C) 1970s
    D) 1990s

29) What decade did the Cornhuskers have the lowest winning percentage (minimum 50 games)?

    A) 1920s
    B) 1940s
    C) 1950s
    D) 1980s

30) How many decades has Nebraska won at least 80 percent of its games (minimum 50 games)?

    A) 2
    B) 3
    C) 4
    D) 5

31) How many Huskers are in the Pro Football Hall of Fame?

    A) 0
    B) 2
    C) 3
    D) 5

32) Who was the most recent team to return a kickoff for a touchdown against Nebraska?

    A) Missouri
    B) Pittsburgh
    C) Texas A&M
    D) Kansas State

33) What was the largest-ever margin of victory for Nebraska in a bowl game?

    A)   28 points
    B)   34 points
    C)   49 points
    D)   54 points

34) What was Nebraska's worst-ever defeat suffered in a bowl game?

    A)   21 points
    B)   27 points
    C)   34 points
    D)   38 points

35) What year did NU play its first-ever night home game?

    A)   1971
    B)   1979
    C)   1983
    D)   1986

36) How many times has Nebraska appeared in the Orange/Sugar/Fiesta/Rose bowls combined?

    A)   24
    B)   29
    C)   31
    D)   33

37) What was the highest winning percentage of an NU head coach who lasted only one season (minimum 5 games)?

    A) .667
    B) .710
    C) .727
    D) .750

38) Who is the only Nebraska quarterback to win the Johnny Unitas Golden Arm Award?

    A) Tommie Frazier
    B) Turner Gill
    C) Eric Crouch
    D) Zac Taylor

39) How many fullbacks from Nebraska are in the College Football Hall of Fame?

    A) 0
    B) 1
    C) 2
    D) 4

40) How many Cornhuskers have won the Lombardi Award?

    A) 1
    B) 3
    C) 5
    D) 7

41) Who is the only Nebraska player to win the Davey O'Brien Award?

    A) Jammal Lord
    B) Turner Gill
    C) Tommie Frazier
    D) Eric Crouch

42) Who was the first Cornhusker to have his jersey number retired?

    A) Rich Glover
    B) Johnny Rodgers
    C) Tom Novak
    D) Bob Brown

43) Who was the first Husker to win the Outland Trophy?

    A) Larry Jacobson
    B) Dave Rimington
    C) Rik Bonness
    D) Will Shields

44) From which of these states have the most Husker All-Americans hailed?

    A) California
    B) Texas
    C) Ohio
    D) Florida

45) Prior to 2007, when was the last season Nebraska lost more than two games at home?

    A) 1951
    B) 1957
    C) 1963
    D) 1968

46) Where did Nebraska Coach Bo Pelini play college football?

    A) Purdue
    B) Louisiana State
    C) Ohio State
    D) Did not play college football

47) Tom Osborne was the first coach in college football history to retire as a reigning National Champion.

    A) True
    B) False

48) What is the record for the fewest total yards allowed in a single game by a Husker defense?

    A) 6
    B) 19
    C) 24
    D) 31

49) Which former Nebraska head coach played QB at Michigan and led the Wolverines to a National Championship in 1948?

    A) Pete Elliott
    B) Bill Jennings
    C) Bill Glassford
    D) Bernie Masterson

50) When was the last time a Nebraska game ended in a tie?

    A) 1972
    B) 1978
    C) 1985
    D) 1991

Darin Erstad started off 1995 by winning an NCAA National Championship as the punter for the 13-0 Nebraska football team. Later that year he batted .410 with 19 HRs and 79 RBIs for the Husker baseball team, earning First Team All-American and becoming a finalist for the Golden Spikes Award as the nation's best player. Erstad finished his Nebraska baseball career as the all-time hits leader with 261, and was selected No. 1 overall in the MLB Draft by the then California Angels. Three years later, Erstad played in his first All-Star game (1998). In 2000, Erstad hit .355 and led the AL in hits (240) on the way to his second All-Star game. He also earned a Silver Slugger Award and a Gold Glove as an outfielder that year. In 2002, Erstad helped the then Anaheim Angels win the World Series, picking up his second Gold Glove as an outfielder along the way. In 2004, Erstad won a third Gold Glove, this time as a first baseman. In doing so, Erstad became the first player in MLB history to win a Gold Glove as an outfielder and as an infielder.

1) B – USC (The Huskers are 0-3-1 all time versus the Trojans.)

2) A – 10 (The Nebraska defense intercepted 10 opponent passes in 2011.)

3) C – 8 (Devaney led the Huskers to eight Big 8 Titles in his 11 seasons as head coach.)

4) C – 6 (Nebraska compiled a 6–3 record in nine bowl games under Devaney.)

5) B – 27 (Irving Fryar wore jersey No. 27 for the Huskers.)

6) A – 379 (Nebraska scored 379 points in 2011, a 29.2 points per game average.)

7) D – Taylor Martinez (Martinez rushed for 241 yards on 15 carries versus Kansas State Oct. 7, 2010.)

8) B – 1976 (Nebraska beat Texas Tech 27-24 in the Astro-Blue Bonnet Bowl inside the Astrodome in Houston, Texas.)

9) D – Clete Pillen (Pillen had 30 total tackles vs. Oklahoma State on Nov. 6, 1976 [Nebraska 14, Oklahoma State 10].)

10) C – 1996 (The Huskers were shut out 0-19 on Sept. 21 at Arizona State.)

11) A – Louisiana Tech (Louisiana Tech passed for 590 yards on Aug. 29, 1998 [Nebraska 56, Louisiana Tech 27].)

12) B – 35 (The Huskers recorded 35 shutouts in Osborne's 25 seasons.)

13) C – 5 (1975, 1976, 1980, 1988 and 1994)

14) A – Mike Rozier (Rozier had 275 carries for 2,148 yards in 1983.)

15) A – Yes (NU backs accomplished this feat at Baylor on Oct. 13, 2001 [IB Thunder Collins 165 yards, IB Daharran Diedrick 137 yards, QB Eric Crouch 132 yards, and FB Judd Davies 119 yards].)

16) D – Mark Schellen (Schellen started at fullback in 1983 and rushed for nine TDs.)

17) B – Ahman Green (Green rushed for 1,086 yards on 141 carries as a true freshman in 1995.)

18) B – 1955 (Nebraska lost to Duke 34–7 on Jan. 1, 1955.)

19) B – 26

20) A – Trev Alberts (Alberts won the Butkus Award as the nation's best linebacker in 1993.)

21) C – 28 (Bo Pelini became the 28th head coach at Nebraska in December 2007.)

22) D – E.O. Stiehm (Stiehm compiled a .913 winning percentage at Nebraska with a 35-2-3 record from 1911-15.)

23) C – W.C. Booth and Tom Osborne (W.C. Booth [.845, record of 46-8-1] and Tom Osborne [.836, record of 255-49-3])

24) A – 0 (The Cornhuskers had no overtime games in 2011.)

25) C – 3 (Crouch had three catches for 109 yards and two TDs in his Nebraska career.)

26) A – Yes (Nebraska has complied an 846-349-40 record, and are one of only 11 schools with 800 or more wins.)

27) D – Jerry Tagge (Tagge was drafted eleventh overall by Green Bay in 1972.)

28) D – 1990s (The Huskers went 108-16-1 for a .864 winning percentage.)

29) B – 1940s (The Huskers went 34-57-0 for a .374 winning percentage.)

30) B – 3 (The Huskers had a winning percentage of .820 in the 1970s, .837 in the 1980s and .864 in the 1990s)

31) C – 3 (Guy Chamberlin, Roy "Link" Lyman and Bob Brown)

32) D – Kansas State (Brandon Banks returned a kickoff 98 yards for a TD in 2008.)

33) C – 49 points (Nebraska beat Northwestern 66-17 in the 2000 Alamo Bowl.)

34) B – 27 points (This happened twice: NU lost 7-34 vs. Duke in the 1955 Orange Bowl and 7-34 vs. Alabama in the 1966 Sugar Bowl.)

35) D – 1986 (Nebraska beat Florida State 34-17 under the lights in the 1986 opener.)

36) B – 29 (17 times in the Orange Bowl, four in the Sugar, six in the Fiesta and two in the Rose Bowl)

37) C – .727 (Fielding Yost was 8-3 in 1898.)

38) A – Tommie Frazier (1995)

39) C – 2 (George Sauer [1931-33] inducted in 1954 and Sam Francis [1934-36] inducted in 1977)

40) C – 5 (Rich Glover 1972, Dave Rimington 1982, Dean Steinkuhler 1983, Grant Wistrom 1997 and Ndamukong Suh 2009)

41) D – Eric Crouch (Crouch won the award for best collegiate quarterback in 2001.)

42) C – Tom Novak (A four-time All-Big 7 choice and 1949 All-American, he had his No. 60 permanently retired after the 1949 season.)

43) A – Larry Jacobson (Jacobson won the first of Nebraska's 8 Outland Trophies in 1971.)

44) B – Texas (Ten Cornhusker All-Americans hailed from the state of Texas, collecting a total of 13 awards between them.)

45) D – 1968 (The Huskers compiled a 2-3 record at home.)

46) C – Ohio State (Pelini was a four-year letterman at safety 1987-90, three-time Academic All-Big Ten, and a Buckeye Captain in 1990.)

47) A – True (Osborne's last game was a 42-17 win vs. Tennessee in the Orange Bowl, which earned Nebraska a share of the National Championship.)

48) D – 31 (NU allowed -17 rushing, 48 passing vs. South Dakota on Sept. 24, 1949. Nebraska won 33-6.)

49) A – Pete Elliott (Elliott led Michigan to a 9-0 record and was named an All-American.)

50) D – 1991 (Nebraska and Colorado played to a 19-19 tie at Colorado on Nov. 2, 1991.)

Note: All answers are valid as of the end of the 2011 season, unless otherwise indicated in the question itself.

1) Which Husker has rushed for the most yards in a single game?

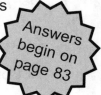

Answers begin on page 83

   A) Ahman Green
   B) Roy Helu Jr.
   C) Mike Rozier
   D) Calvin Jones

2) How many times has Nebraska finished the season ranked in the Top 5 of the AP Poll?

   A) 12
   B) 14
   C) 16
   D) 18

3) Who was the first Husker to rush for 200 yards in a game?

   A) Roger Craig
   B) Mike Rozier
   C) Frank Solich
   D) I.M. Hipp

4) Who is Nebraska's only two-time unanimous All-American?

   A) Dave Rimington
   B) Bob Brown
   C) Johnny Rodgers
   D) Mike Rozier

5) Who is Nebraska's career sacks leader?

    A)   Jim Skow
    B)   Grant Wistrom
    C)   Broderick Thomas
    D)   Trev Alberts

6) What are the most rushing yards a Nebraska defense has given up in a single game?

    A)   478
    B)   506
    C)   567
    D)   590

7) Which Nebraska kicker made the most field goals in his career?

    A)   Kris Brown
    B)   Josh Brown
    C)   Gregg Barrios
    D)   Alex Henery

8) Who holds Nebraska's record for the longest punt?

    A)   Kyle Larson
    B)   Sam Koch
    C)   Mike Stigge
    D)   Darin Erstad

9) Who holds the Husker record for the longest punt return?

    A)   DeJuan Groce
    B)   Bobby Newcombe
    C)   Johnny Rodgers
    D)   Irving Fryar

10) Has Nebraska ever rushed for more than 650 yards as a team in a single game?

    A)   Yes
    B)   No

Cornhuskerology Trivia Challenge

1) B – Roy Helu Jr. (Helu rushed for 307 yards on 28 carries versus Missouri in 2010.)

2) B – 14 (Nebraska has finished in the AP Top-5 14 times. Most recently was in 1999 when they finished third.)

3) C – Frank Solich (Solich rushed for 204 yards at Air Force on Sept. 25, 1965 [Neb 27, Air Force 17].)

4) A – Dave Rimington (Unanimous choice in 1981-82)

5) D – Trev Alberts (Alberts recorded 29.5 sacks for Nebraska from 1990-93.)

6) B – 506 (The Sooners piled up 506 rushing yards at Oklahoma on Nov. 24, 1956 [Neb 6, OU 54].)

7) D – Alex Henery (68 FGs on 76 attempts from 2007-10)

8) C – Mike Stigge (Stigge booted an 87-yarder on Oct. 10, 1992, vs. Oklahoma State [Nebraska 55, Oklahoma State 0].)

9) B – Bobby Newcombe (Newcombe had a 94-yard touchdown return vs. Missouri on Sept. 30, 2000 [Nebraska 42, Missouri 24].)

10) A – Yes (The Huskers had 677 yards on Sept. 18, 1982, vs. New Mexico State [Neb 68, NM State 0].)

Note: All answers are valid as of the end of the 2011 season, unless otherwise indicated in the question itself.

Player / Team Score Sheet

Name:_____

First Quarter			Second Quarter			Third Quarter			Fourth Quarter			Overtime Bonus	
1		26		1		26		1		26		1		26		1	
2		27		2		27		2		27		2		27		2	
3		28		3		28		3		28		3		28		3	
4		29		4		29		4		29		4		29		4	
5		30		5		30		5		30		5		30		5	
6		31		6		31		6		31		6		31		6	
7		32		7		32		7		32		7		32		7	
8		33		8		33		8		33		8		33		8	
9		34		9		34		9		34		9		34		9	
10		35		10		35		10		35		10		35		10	
11		36		11		36		11		36		11		36			
12		37		12		37		12		37		12		37			
13		38		13		38		13		38		13		38			
14		39		14		39		14		39		14		39			
15		40		15		40		15		40		15		40			
16		41		16		41		16		41		16		41			
17		42		17		42		17		42		17		42			
18		43		18		43		18		43		18		43			
19		44		19		44		19		44		19		44			
20		45		20		45		20		45		20		45			
21		46		21		46		21		46		21		46			
22		47		22		47		22		47		22		47			
23		48		23		48		23		48		23		48			
24		49		24		49		24		49		24		49			
25		50		25		50		25		50		25		50			

____ x 1 =____   ____ x 2 =____   ____ x 3 =____   ____ x 4 =____   ____ x 4 =____

Multiply total number correct by point value/quarter to calculate totals for each quarter.

Add total of all quarters below.

Total Points:_____

Thank you for playing *Cornhuskerology Trivia Challenge*.

Additional score sheets are available at:
www.TriviaGameBooks.com

Player / Team Score Sheet

Name:_____

First Quarter			Second Quarter			Third Quarter			Fourth Quarter			Overtime Bonus	
1	26		1	26		1	26		1	26		1	
2	27		2	27		2	27		2	27		2	
3	28		3	28		3	28		3	28		3	
4	29		4	29		4	29		4	29		4	
5	30		5	30		5	30		5	30		5	
6	31		6	31		6	31		6	31		6	
7	32		7	32		7	32		7	32		7	
8	33		8	33		8	33		8	33		8	
9	34		9	34		9	34		9	34		9	
10	35		10	35		10	35		10	35		10	
11	36		11	36		11	36		11	36			
12	37		12	37		12	37		12	37			
13	38		13	38		13	38		13	38			
14	39		14	39		14	39		14	39			
15	40		15	40		15	40		15	40			
16	41		16	41		16	41		16	41			
17	42		17	42		17	42		17	42			
18	43		18	43		18	43		18	43			
19	44		19	44		19	44		19	44			
20	45		20	45		20	45		20	45			
21	46		21	46		21	46		21	46			
22	47		22	47		22	47		22	47			
23	48		23	48		23	48		23	48			
24	49		24	49		24	49		24	49			
25	50		25	50		25	50		25	50			
___ x 1 =____			___ x 2 =____			___ x 3 =____			___ x 4 =____			___ x 4 =____	

Multiply total number correct by point value/quarter to calculate totals for each quarter.

Add total of all quarters below.

Total Points:_____

Thank you for playing *Cornhuskerology Trivia Challenge*.

**Additional score sheets are available at:
www.TriviaGameBooks.com**